Little
LIBRARIES,
Big HEROES

MIRANDA PAUL

Illustrated by
JOHN PARRA

CLARION BOOKS
Houghton Mifflin Harcourt
Boston New York

FOR THOUSANDS OF YEARS,

people have loved stories about heroes.

Mythical heroes, historical heroes, and even . . .

. . . ordinary heroes.

Like this guy: Todd. (Pretty ordinary, right?)

Here's kid-Todd, *pretending* to be a superhero.

In school, he didn't feel heroic. Even though his mother had been a teacher who loved books, reading was difficult for him. He was often scolded for asking too many questions, and was told that he wasn't a good student.

Todd's mom disagreed. She told him he was gifted and had something big to offer the world. "You could do anything," she said. He hoped she was right.

Todd studied hard, graduated from school, and got a job.
At work, Todd discovered that he liked helping others. But then
his mother died, and he became the one who needed help to get
through sad times. He missed her terribly.

Memories of his mom teaching neighborhood kids how to
read gave Todd an idea.

He cut up an old door and hammered the pieces together
to make a tiny one-room schoolhouse. He stacked books inside,
nailed a sign on the front, and placed the little library on his
lawn. Now he could share his mother's love of reading with
anyone who passed by.

There was just one problem . . . Very few people passed by.

One day, during a rummage sale,
Todd's neighbors spotted his creation.

Todd told them about his mom. People loved his story. It reminded them of ordinary heroes they knew.

Soon, neighbors who had never met before were gathered around, chatting like old friends. They grabbed books. They gave books. The little library became the center of their neighborhood.

Todd felt his nifty box of books had *potential*. He called up his friend Rick, who was always chock-full of grand ideas.

Rick thought that they could build thousands of little boxes!

Like Andrew Carnegie, who once built 2,510 libraries!

They could take trips!

Like Lutie Stearns, who brought traveling libraries all over Wisconsin!

Lutie

Stearns

"WAIT A MINUTE!" Todd said.

Andrew Carnegie had been a wealthy businessman. Lutie Stearns was a trained librarian. The two of them were just **ordinary** guys. (And they were particularly low on cash.)

How many libraries could two **ordinary** guys create?

How far could **ordinary** people spread an idea?

They agreed on one thing— they wanted to find out.

For months they salvaged, designed, sawed, and painted.

They learned important skills, such as how to recycle a barn, how to pick out a sliver, and how to convince family members that sawing and painting were fun.

The team lined up their finished masterpieces and waited for the crowds.

But . . .

crowds didn't come.

Only *one* person bought a little library.

The freshly built libraries sat.

And sat.

And sat.

The team's spirits withered as they waited.

Books are filled with great ideas, they knew, but those ideas could only spread if people actually read them. So Todd and Rick decided that if people wouldn't come get the libraries, they'd bring the libraries to the people.

LTL LBRY

Out they went with thirty tiny libraries, planting them like seeds between Madison, Chicago, and Minneapolis.

Just like at the rummage sale, folks gathered around. Curiosity lured readers to the little boxes. They borrowed and shared books.

Main

First

Friends and neighbors talked with other friends and neighbors (who talked with more friends and neighbors) about the books they'd read and where they'd gotten them.

It was working!

The seeds of Todd and Rick's idea were beginning to grow. A radio interview spread the word about the little free libraries all around Wisconsin. Then a national TV show featured their idea. The whole country seemed to be buzzing about the tiny, anything-but-ordinary libraries.

Over the next year, four hundred little libraries sprang up across the United States. Each library needed a caretaker, called a *steward*. Stewards were ordinary citizens—some were even kids. Many of them wouldn't stay ordinary, though—they became **community heroes.**

After Hurricane Katrina devastated her hometown of New Orleans, a six-year-old girl named Nikki collected nearly two thousand books. She gave a box of books to every Little Free Library in the city. Then she wrote a letter to Todd and Rick's organization asking for a little library of her own, and she got one!

Nikki tucked some of her favorite books inside, and people have been checking out stories from it ever since.

In El Paso, near the US—Mexico border, reading programs were short on money. A librarian named Ms. López placed the first Little Free Library in Texas at an elementary school there. With her students' help, the idea spread to more than fifty locations around the city. Soon, families had more access to books in English and Spanish.

In Western Uganda, volunteers set up a primary school and a Little Free Library within a refugee camp. The women, men, and children who lived there had escaped great violence and had been forced to leave most of their possessions behind. Some of them learned to read from the magazines and picture books they found inside the tiny library.

As the libraries spread around the world,
more tales of **ordinary heroes** emerged . . .

from within a Wisconsin prison, along a hiking trail
in Canada, and in cities across Brazil.

Stewards placed Little Free Libraries at a hospital in
Ireland, on a street corner in Pakistan, outside a house in
South Korea, and near a schoolyard in South Sudan.

LITTLE FREE LIBRARY

Today, thousands of ordinary (and creative!) heroes are bringing millions of free books to their friends and neighbors.

Today, those friends and neighbors will share them with other friends and neighbors.

Today, books will be loved. Big ideas will spark.

And tomorrow—

LITTLE FREE LIBRARY

—who knows?

Tomorrow might bring another
hero story, written by

YOU...

and shared with the whole wide
book-loving world.

AUTHOR'S NOTE

When I'm working on a nonfiction story, I tend to find out more information than will ever fit into one picture book. Such was the case with *Little Libraries, Big Heroes*. Through reading articles and conducting personal interviews with the cofounders and stewards of Little Free Library, there was a common theme—the power of books.

Books have helped me get through tough times as well as gain a better understanding of our world. As a young student, I attended schools with only a small library, or no library, and no certified librarian. As a teacher, I've worked in places where my students have had limited access to free books. So when I came across a Little Free Library in 2011, I found the idea remarkable.

While researching, I learned that many "ordinary" people are responsible for the extraordinary movement that has become Little Free Library (LFL). By bringing books to their own neighborhoods, stewards' little libraries became meeting places. New friendships, ideas, and projects sprang to life as a result—including solutions to serious problems that arose from violence or disaster. For example, while out playing Pokémon GO in a local park, Gregory Wheeler became the victim of a shooting. He passed time in his hospital bed by coming up with ideas to improve his community in Columbus, Ohio. After his recovery, he designed the rocket-shaped LFL #61550 to "give the neighborhood kids some inspiration to look towards a brighter future."

Builders and caretakers of these libraries have shown incredible creativity. Building materials have included an old TV set, a telephone booth, newspaper vending machines, a medicine cabinet, a mini-refrigerator, electronic waste, Lego bricks, and even a large block of ice!

I was delighted to learn that many LFL stewards are children. I will never cease to be amazed and inspired by young people who let passion fuel their good work. Research has shown that reading fosters empathy. To witness a global movement of grownups and young people committed to a culture of reading is encouraging and empowering. Long live books and the ordinary heroes who write, read, and share them!

If you would like to become a steward and bring the joy of books to your community, visit littlefreelibrary.org to get started.

MORE ABOUT LITTLE FREE LIBRARIES

A Little Free Library is a registered container that houses free books for exchange, with the current motto "Take a Book, Share a Book." The libraries are put in highly visible places—along curbs or sidewalks, on school property, near businesses, etc. A library can look however the owner wants it to look. Anyone can build one, but those who plan to use the name Little Free Library must have an official charter sign and number on the library. A volunteer steward (AKA community hero) makes sure the library stays in good condition and rotates or restocks the collection of books regularly.

MORE ABOUT THE PEOPLE AND EVENTS IN THIS BOOK

Todd Bol (1956-2018) and Rick Brooks are the cofounders of Little Free Library, but there are many ordinary people who have provided—and continue to provide—inspiration and support to their organization, beginning with Todd's mother, June Bol. Amish carpenter Henry Miller helped build the first set of libraries out of wood from a barn destroyed by a tornado, and Todd's wife, Susan; his brother Tony; and his children, Allison and Austin, pitched in. Nikki Leali brought thousands of free books to New Orleans when she was just six years old. She's been maintaining LFL #1757 for years. In El Paso, Lisa M. López-Williamson is the librarian who installed the first LFL (#1175) in Texas, and helped form the group that now has built more than 150 LFLs along the border. Volunteer Jeanne Ratzloff and Ugandan project manager Benson Wereje are two of the people who helped install a Little Free Library (#4996) at the Kyangwali Refugee Settlement.

Todd Bol was in second grade when his mother gave him the encouraging words he'd hold on to for the rest of his life. It wasn't until 2009—about forty-five years later—that Todd made the first little library and placed it on his lawn in Hudson, Wisconsin. In 2010, the first requested library outside of Todd's hometown was installed on a bike path in Madison, Wisconsin. Although the early libraries were self-funded and given away for free, people and the media spread the word—and there were four hundred Little Free Libraries by the end of 2011. The organization became an official nonprofit a few months later, and donations rolled in. By August 2012, the idea had spread beyond the United States, with a total of 2,510 libraries worldwide. When this very sentence was written, there were more than 75,000 registered LFLs in eighty-eight countries around the world. All of the locations mentioned in this story describe actual libraries.

TO LEARN MORE

Aldrich, Margret. *The Little Free Library Book*. Minneapolis: Coffee House Press, 2015.

  Includes 250 pages of information about the history of the organization, stories and photos from around the world, and ideas and tips for building libraries.

Rau, Dana Meachen. *Andrew Carnegie: Captain of Industry*. North Mankato, MN: Compass Point Books, 2005.

  A middle grade biography of Andrew Carnegie, a man known for his donation of money to build libraries as well as educational and scientific institutions.

Stotts, Stuart. *Books in a Box: Lutie Stearns and the Traveling Libraries of Wisconsin*. DeForest, WI: Big Valley Press, 2005.

  A fictionalized biography of Wisconsin's traveling librarian, Lutie Stearns, drawn from correspondence, magazine articles, and other historical accounts from the late 1800s and early 1900s.

www.littlefreelibrary.org

  The official website of Little Free Library includes a map of library locations, images of some of the most creative libraries, links to contact the organization's staff, and more.

"You can be the story of change." —Todd H. Bol

For Sharon, Molly, and Robert "Bookmobile Bob" Ripley—
my childhood library hero —M.P.

For the Santa Barbara and Goleta Public Libraries—my first introduction
into a wider and imaginative world —J.P.

In 2018, as final touches to this book were being made, Little Free Library creator Todd H. Bol was diagnosed with
pancreatic cancer and passed away a very short time after. Stewards around the globe placed white or gray ribbons on their
Little Free Libraries in remembrance. In honor of Todd's legacy, a similar ribbon has been included in one of the illustrations in this book.
May his life and deeds continue to inspire all who read and share books everywhere.

Clarion Books
3 Park Avenue
New York, New York 10016

Clarion Books is an imprint of Houghton Mifflin Harcourt Publishing Company.

hmhbooks.com

The illustrations in this book were done in acrylic paint on illustration board.
The text was set in LunchBox.
Design by Andrea Miller

Little Free Library® is a registered trademark of
Little Free Library, LTD, a 501(c)(3) nonprofit organization.

Library of Congress Cataloging-in-Publication Data
Names: Paul. Miranda. author. | Parra. John. illustrator. Title: Little libraries. big heroes / by Miranda Paul : illustrated by John Parra.
Description: Boston : New York : Clarion Books. Houghton Mifflin Harcourt. [2019] Identifiers: LCCN 2018052000 | ISBN 9780544800274
(hardcover picture book) Subjects: LCSH: Little free libraries—Juvenile literature. | Bol. Todd—Juvenile literature. Classification: LCC Z675.
L59 P38 2019 | DDC 027—dc23 LC record available at https://lccn.loc.gov/2018052000

Manufactured in China
SCP 10 9 8 7 6 5 4 3 2 1
4500761119